Passion.

Samantha Chensee

BookLeaf Publishing

India | USA | UK

Passion. © 2022 Samantha Chensee

All rights reserved.

No part of this publication may be reproduced, stored in a retrieval system, or transmitted, in any form or by any means, electronic, mechanical, photocopying, recording or otherwise, without the prior written permission of the presenters.

Samantha Chensee asserts the moral right to be identified as author of this work.

Presentation by *BookLeaf Publishing*

Web: www.bookleafpub.com

E-mail: info@bookleafpub.com

ISBN: 9789357448048

First edition 2022

A Cry For Help

Are you worth it?
All this pain..
Are you gonna screw me over like the other
guys?
Let me die in the shower if I try to suicide?

You know how I feel
Yet you couldn't care less.
You're just like every other guy
I've ever met.

Use me
Break me
Then throw me away.

You don't see what I see
No one does.
Why do I feel differently?

Are you really the rainbow after the rain?
If not
Then why wont this feeling go away?
~ Samantha Chensee ©

A Dark Hell

I'm locked up,
I can't breathe.
I'm being murdered from the inside,
It's a monster waiting to escape.

All that goes through my mind is your name.
It's repeated continuously.
Your eyes,
They shined as bright as the stars in the night
sky.

Every time I think of you,
Pain courses through my body,
Waiting to escape.
Yet I don't know why I still think of you.

It's because of you,
This eternal pain I endured-
I enjoyed it though,
Because it reminds me of you.

Everything I see reminds me of you,
Your smile is as white as the snow in the Blue
Mountains,
Your hands as warm as the sun,

Your hair as dark as night.

When I think of those things,
The pain starts again.
But I only think of it in the darkness,
This pain.

So enjoyable.
It stabs at me like a knife.
It's 1am and I'm thinking of you.
I'm holding a knife.

"Don't do it, please? I love you." the text reads.
But I don't think.
The knife goes in.
And as I lay, enjoying the pain, I realise
something.

The pain I was experiencing:
Heartbreak.
My heart:
My own personal hell.
~ Samantha Chensee ©

Broken

What's the point of living?
If we don't even talk.
You're shy
I'm shy

So what's the point?
I'm the girl who's "happy" all the time.
A perfect life
Everyone thinks I'm always happy.

Well
You thought wrong.
I'm the girl who pretends.
Who's broken inside

Who ponders self-harm
Who ponders suicide.
I'm the girl you can fuck over many times
But will give you chances you don't even
deserve.

You destroyed me.
And you don't even know it.
~ Samantha Chensee ©

Why Am I Alive?

You don't understand
This never-ending pain
I want to end it all
But I don't have the courage.

Why am I alive?
This feeling of drowning inside
Does it end?
Will I get through this life?

You aren't there for me
So why do I bother staying alive for you?
This feeling I feel, it's because of you.
So why do I bother when you don't even care?

I hide it all behind a mask
I conceal it so well you don't even ask
You can't even see I thought you knew me well
Why am I alive?
If you can't even tell.
~ Samantha Chensee ©

Sunset.

The sunset changes with each passing day,
Yet we never get a say.
The colours collide,
Allowing us to see galaxies with our eyes.

The sun dives into the clouds,
Creating a rainbow of colour,
Of magic and wonder.

Clouds cover the setting sun,
Creating a halo around the colours,
As beautiful as the boy she loved,
As beautiful as a turtle dove.
~ Samantha Chensee ©

Generation Z.

We are screwed up as a generation
Born all different people
Reliant on technology as a means of
communication
A generation lacking trust

Screenshotting everything.
A selfish generation
Who don't know the meaning of the word
sacrifice.
People who claim to be people of faith
Yet don't act like one at all.

A generation where relationships mean nothing
Where relationships are technology based
A judgmental generation
Who screenshots photos, sends them to other
people and judge together.

Why can't we be an accepting generation?
People who accept others for who they are...
Their hobbies
For their flaws

For their true selves.
Why hide behind a mask?
Be who you are
And if people don't like it...

Then tell them to go away.
I was born a selfless person into a generation full
of selfish people.
Sure I am selfish at times
I am human after all

But everyone else is selfish all the time.
Be yourself
Stop hiding behind a fake identity.
Be selflessStop being selfish.

But most importantly...
Be accepting and love everyone.

~ Samantha Chensee ©

Boom.

And I gave you the ammunition:
My heart on a gold platter.

You lit the fuse
And waited.
You acted like you had no intention of hurting
me,
Like you were innocent..

You acted as if you were an angel
Sent down from the heavens
To bless my life.
To show me how every other guy should've
treated me.
To make evident how a king treats his queen.

But a bomb once lit
Eventually explodes.
I prayed that day would never come,
I prayed to God that you weren't a devil in a
disguise,

That I wasn't dancing with the devil...
But oh how wrong was I?
~ Samantha Chensee ©

Release.

Cry
Don't hold it in
Let the emotion take a hold of you
Let all the pain

The hurt
The anger
Let it all out.
Let your tears tell everyone how hurt you are.

How their actions and words
Have impacted you.
Don't let it consume you.
Open the bottle

And let the contents cause a flood
So anything dead can be revived
The once brown, dead grass is now fresh with
life.
The drought-stricken rivers have been touched
and filled.

You see…
Anything on the brink of death

Can be healed,
And given another chance at life.
~ Samantha Chensee ©

Worth.

Darling he was never worth it,
He was never worth your love
Or the river of tears that flowed from you.

You'll find the one who is worth it.
Who will give you the world and
Who is worthy of your love.

So wait for the one
Who proves to you that
He is one of a kind.

Who will fight to
Pry open the gate that guards your heart
And protect it from the world.
~ Samantha Chensee ©

Love Kills.

Love.
It hurts as much as getting shot in the heart.
Yet you still love…
But why?

His eyes are as blue as the ocean.
But why you of all people?
You've broken me once,
You may do it again.

You ignore me, so I ignore you.
But seeing you happy just kills me.
Seeing you talk to other girls makes me want to
punch them in the face.
Can you not see me?

Do you not notice me?
I sit alone in the dark corner, holding a knife.
"Do it." Says my brain.
But do I have the courage?

Do I have the wits?
No. The hurt. The lies.
Did you not see the tears in my eyes?
Are you blind?

Your muscles are as big as a blue whales,
I love 'em more than I loved you.
They say that love is blind,
But you're constantly on my mind.

"I love you." You whisper,
but was that all a lie?
I don't know anymore,
I just want to die.

My heart is constantly aching,
I want to end it all.
My last words will be:
Love kills, that's all.
~ Samantha Chensee ©

Never Lasting.

My little world started to reveal itself to me…
The truth… the hurtful truth.
That… no matter how hard I try
Happiness is an emotion that never lasts.

My little world showed the true harshness of
everything around me.
No matter how hard I try
No matter how happy someone says they are
They will never truly be happy.

Happiness will last
For a certain amount of time
A day
A week

A month
A year
A second.
Because…

The reality is…
That
No matter how happy someone says they are

Happiness is a condition that never lasts.
~ Samantha Chensee ©

Losing Myself.

I don't know who I am anymore
I'm a stranger in my own body.
I lost my way…
You controlled me

My life
Revolved around you.
So now?
Now I don't know myself.

The mirror reflects back
My physical form…
That never changed.
But I've never felt so lost

In my own body.
I don't know who I am anymore
I'm a stranger…
The light

Everyone once saw in me
Is dimmed.
The qualities I once possessed
Are gone.

Who I once was
Has changed…
She's gone…
She's lost.
~ Samantha Chensee ©

Death.

Sometimes I wonder what the world would be
like
Or what other people's lives would be like
Without my presence.

Would it be a dark place
Or would there be more happiness?
Would everyone forget about me
Or would it be like I didn't exist?

Then I remember
The promises I made to those closest to me,
And the way other people's deaths
Have affected those around them,

And the ever-present darkness within their souls.
Thus, making me wish that
Death and emotions would cease to exist,
So I may leave this world

Without the burden of knowing
That my death plunged once
Colourful souls
Into darkness.
~ Samantha Chensee ©

Forgiveness.

Why
Why did you turn my heart into sand?
Why did you ruin everything we ever had?
Don't try to blame this shit on me

Cause you know you're at fault.
But even to this day
You can't answer my questions.
I doubt you know the answers yourself.

Why did you compare me to other girls you
met?
Why did you decide after being with me for so
long that I wasn't good enough for you?
That we weren't meant to be?
What suddenly changed your mind?

I know
I'm imperfect…
But you were too.
I accepted you for you.

I forgave you for all your mistakes
For lying to me
And dragging me through hell and back

And for never fighting for me.

So
For shattering my heart
For breaking a multitude of promises
For causing me so much anguish and pain

For being the reason a river flowed from my
cheeks
For being a lesson learnt
For making me feel like a last choice
For making me question my own self-worth…

I forgive you.
~ Samantha Chensee ©

Fright.

Fright
A common emotion caused from many things...
Horror movies
The thought of the world ending

Events that occur out of our control
The idea of the inevitable...
But whats the most common idea associated
with fear?
The fear of getting hurt.

Hearts are fragile objects
One touch and they can be shattered into a
million pieces
They cause individuals to care to much for
others more than themselves.
They trigger strong emotions such as

Love
Sadness
Anger and
Frustration.

Once shattered it is difficult to piece together...
But with time it shall heal.

With time it becomes difficult to trust

Hard to let people in
Hard to open up
Due to a fear of becoming hurt again.
So you begin to push people away

Which becomes habit.
You build an iron wall around your heart
Vines growing and wrapping themselves around
the bars with thorns
To guard your heart from the world.

You push everyone away,
Genuine people who care and worry
And eventually...
They give up

They stop fighting for you
And walk away...
Even though you pushed them away,
The thorns pricking fingers every time someone
tried to be let in...

You end up hurt and shattered
And just isolate yourself....
Debating just ending your life so you never feel
pain again.
~ Samantha Chensee ©

Drained.

Mentally drained.
Emotionally drained.
Mentally tired.
Tired of this world

Tired of this life.
I'm a living burden
An annoyance
Someone as annoying as a fly.

I'm mentally screwed.
But you?
Lately you have made my life a living hell.
I hope she tramples your heart

Tears it into a thousand pieces the way you have
mine.
You lied.
Lies babble out of your mouth.
I sit here
Hurt

Wanting to cry
Tears burning the back of my eyes

Emotionless
In a trance.

I feel nothing.I
 hold a knife to my wrist
Cold to the touch.
Nothing

I feel nothing.
Eternal darkness nips at me
Bites at me
One quick slice
Darkness.
~ Samantha Chensee ©

Overwhelm Me.

It's 12:18am and this isn't the first time I've felt
like this.
It's high school all over again.
Uncontrollable thoughts.
Lonely nights of crying myself to sleep.

You don't get the hints
The cries for help
Why can't I just be honest like everyone else?
Why can't I be normal?

No thoughts of holding a blade to my skin
No thoughts of the pain sliding against my
wrists
No thoughts of the blood dripping onto the tiled
floor
No images of red pooling around me

As the life slowly leaves me.
Why can't I be normal?
No relapses
No feelings of loneliness

Of failure
Of feeling like a burden.

It's 12:24am and I sit here in the darkness
Lonely
Holding a knife with a new blade
Who's sharp point catches the light.

"I love you all. Sorry for ever entering your lives
in the first place. This world is better off without
me." my final message reads.
I hold the blade to my skin and press
Feeling the blood gush out of my veins
And a feeling of relief along with it.
~ Samantha Chensee ©

Never Too Late.

Never Too Late.

They say that you can always save a person's
life
That you're "never too late"…
But what people don't realise is how much
emotions can control an individual's thoughts
and actions
With one swipe of a knife.

With one jump into a river
One last breath taken under water
One knot
A life can be taken.

So you see…
You can be too late
A second late
A millisecond late.

Within a few minutes or seconds that persons
life can end…
And the thought that you could have saved them
will haunt you forever.
~ Samantha Chensee ©